Educators Love STEP-UP E
So Do Children.*

In this exciting series:

- THE WORDS ARE HARDER (but not too hard)
- THERE'S A LOT MORE TEXT (but it's in bigger print)
- THERE ARE PLENTY OF ILLUSTRATIONS (but they are not just picture books)
- And the subject matter has been carefully chosen to appeal to young readers who want to find out about the world for themselves. These informative and lively books are just the answer.

*"STEP-UP BOOKS

. . . fill a need for precise informational material written in a simple readable form which children can and will enjoy. More please!"—EVELYN L. HEADLEY, *Director of Elementary Education, Edison, New Jersey.*

"I love them."—STEVE MEYER, *second grade pupil, Chicago, Illinois.*

Meet ROBERT E. LEE is the story of a great American leader forced to make a terrible decision. Robert E. Lee the Virginian, son of a Revolutionary hero, served in the U.S. Army as America moved towards Civil War. Loving his country, he hated to see the Union split, but he could not fight against the South. His agonizing decision, his brilliant military leadership, and the fine example he set when the battle was done, are all recounted in this thoroughly researched and richly illustrated book.

GEORGE TROW was born in Greenwich, Connecticut, and went to Harvard University where he was president of *The Harvard Lampoon.* He has lived in New York City for most of his life, and now writes for *The New Yorker.*

Mr. Trow became interested in Robert E. Lee during a stay in Tidewater Virginia, and pursued the Lee legend in many parts of the state. *Meet Robert E. Lee* is Mr. Trow's first children's book.

TED LEWIN was born in Buffalo, New York. He studied art at Pratt Institute, supporting himself there by wrestling professionally.

Illustrations by Mr. Lewin have appeared in many magazines and books, including the Random House *Look-It-Up Book of Presidents.*

Mr. Lewin is married and lives in Brooklyn, New York. He likes to scuba dive, and keeps a collection of exotic tropical fish.

BOOK CLUB EDITION

MEET
ROBERT E. LEE

by George Swift Trow
illustrated by Ted Lewin

To my mother, Anne Carter Trow

Published in the United States by Random House, Inc., New York, and simultaneously
in Canada by Random House of Canada Limited, Toronto.
Library of Congress Catalog Card Number: 69-18097
Manufactured in the United States of America

A B C D E F G H I 3 4 5

1
Meet Robert E. Lee

Robert E. Lee was a great general. He was one of the greatest generals in American history. But for four terrible years, General Lee fought against the United States.

Robert E. Lee came from Virginia. His family had lived in Virginia for over 150 years. The first Lees in America had come from England. Virginia was called a colony then. It belonged to England. There were 13 English colonies in America.

But after many years people in the colonies felt they were no longer English. They felt they were Americans. They did not want to be ruled by the English King.

On July 4, 1776, leaders of the colonies met. They agreed to sign the Declaration of Independence. The Declaration said the colonies did not belong to England any more.

Two Lees signed the Declaration.

The colonies asked a Virginia soldier to lead their armies. His name was George Washington.

England did not want the 13 colonies to break away. An English army was sent to America.

Robert E. Lee's father was a great general in the war with England. "Light Horse Harry" Lee became a hero of the American Revolution.

Harry Lee Attacks: August, 1777

200 English soldiers rode out of the woods into an open field. They shouted and laughed as they rode. Suddenly shots rang out. Englishmen fell from their horses.

Out of the woods came Light Horse Harry Lee and 60 Virginia horsemen. They attacked! More English soldiers fell.

Harry Lee won a great battle. He took many prisoners. He brought them to General George Washington. Washington said Light Horse Harry was one of America's best soldiers.

The war lasted four more years. At last the Americans won. The 13 colonies became a new country, the United States of America. George Washington of Virginia was the first President. And Harry Lee was the first governor of Virginia.

2
Boyhood in Virginia

It was a fine summer day 28 years after the Revolution. A battered old coach rolled down a long driveway. Inside was Harry Lee's wife, Ann Carter Lee. With her were the children, Charles, Smith and Annie.

And on her lap sat her little boy, Robert. He was three years old.

Harry Lee was taking his family away from Stratford, the great brick house of the Lees.

After the Revolution, things had been hard for Light Horse Harry. The famous soldier had tried to make money. But he had lost the money he had. He had even been sent to jail because he could not pay back money he had borrowed.

And so there had been bad days at Stratford after Robert E. Lee was born. No one farmed the land. Few friends visited.

Now the Lees had to leave. It cost too much to live in the big house.

It was hard to leave. Stratford was one of the finest houses in Virginia. Lees had lived there for almost 100 years. In one room both the Lees who signed the Declaration of Independence had been born. And in 1807, Robert E. Lee had been born in that same room.

Harry Lee had to leave Stratford. But he could not leave Virginia. He loved his state. Once he had said, "Virginia is my country."

So the family moved to Alexandria, a small town of brick houses in Virginia. It was near Washington, the new capital of the United States.

But Light Horse Harry could not stay long. Things went wrong again.

One of his friends was attacked by a mob. Harry tried to help and was badly hurt. He almost died. The American government sent the old hero to a far-off island to get well. But he never did. And he never saw his family again. He died a few years later on his way home to Virginia.

Mrs. Lee and the children lived in a small house now. But Robert was happy. There was green Virginia country all around. Robert could ride and hunt, or swim in the river.

When Robert was 13, Charles went to work and Smith joined the Navy. Now Robert was head of the family. He had to take care of his mother and sisters.

Mrs. Lee was often sick. Robert took care of her after school. Often he carried her to her coach. The Lee's Negro coachman, Nat, would drive them around Alexandria.

Many things in the town made Robert think of his father and the Revolution. He went to the church George Washington had gone to. People told stories about George Washington and Light Horse Harry in the war. Robert heard about Washington's funeral.

Light Horse Harry had spoken there. He had said Washington was "First in war, first in peace, first in the hearts of his countrymen."

Robert wanted to be like his father and the great Washington.

Robert decided to go to West Point, the United States Military Academy. After four years there he would be an army officer. And West Point was free. This would help the Lees. They had very little money.

But it was hard to get into West Point. Robert worked hard. People sent letters to the government. They said he should go. His teacher called him a fine student and a gentleman. Robert got in.

3
At West Point

Many young soldiers in fine uniforms stood in long rows. A famous French general had come to see the cadets at West Point.

It was July, 1825. Robert E. Lee had come to the Academy just a month before. Today he was in dress uniform for the first time.

It was an exciting day for Robert. The famous Frenchman was General Lafayette. He had fought in the American Revolution. He had helped George Washington and Light Horse Harry beat the English.

Robert had already met Lafayette. A few months before, the great man had visited Alexandria. After a big celebration he had called on the Lees. Robert was very proud.

Now Robert was at West Point to learn to be a soldier like Lafayette.

West Point was in New York. It was a beautiful place on the Hudson River. But life was hard for the cadets. The buildings were old and uncomfortable. The work was hard.

Cadet Lee got up at dawn. He had to study all morning and march on the parade field after lunch. But he liked to work. He found science and drawing fun. He even liked to march. The life of a soldier pleased him.

In two years Robert was allowed to go home and visit his mother. He was sad to find her very sick. But it was good to be home. He was glad to see his old friends again.

The last two years at the Academy were the hardest. Robert's class started with 87 boys in it. Only half finished. Robert did very well. Just one cadet got better marks. And he and Robert were chosen to lead all the cadets at West Point.

When Robert was 21 he graduated from West Point and came home. He was an engineer in the Army now. His work was building forts.

Mrs. Lee was very, very sick. Robert gave her medicine and sat by her bed. But before long she died.

Robert was sad. He would miss his mother very much.

After Mrs. Lee died, her coachman, Nat, had nowhere to go. He was old and sick. Robert wanted to help him. When the Army sent Robert to build a fort in Georgia, he took Nat with him. The warm weather would help the old man get better.

4
Marriage

Soon after Mrs. Lee died, Robert began to visit a girl named Mary Custis. Her father was George Washington Parke Custis. He was George Washington's adopted son. The Custis family lived at Arlington, a large house near Alexandria.

When Robert could get away from Georgia, he often visited Arlington.

Before long, Robert asked Mary to marry him. Mr. Custis was a rich man. He was not sure his only child should marry a poor army officer. But Mary wanted to marry Robert. At last her father agreed. On a rainy day in 1831, Robert E. Lee married Mary Custis at Arlington.

The Army had given Robert a new job. He had to work at Fort Monroe, in Hampton Roads, Virginia. Robert and Mary went to live there.

A few days later, horrible things happened near by. First, angry Negroes went from farm to farm killing white people.

Then soldiers from Fort Monroe were sent out to get them. Almost 100 black people were killed. Many of them had done nothing.

Weeks later the black leader, Nat Turner, was caught and hanged.

Turner had been angry at white men for making black men slaves.

Many Negroes had been brought from Africa to be slaves in the South. They were made to work in the fields. They had to work in white people's houses without pay.

Some white people were cruel to slaves. People like the Lees took good care of them. But no slave had a good life. It was a terrible thing to be owned by another man.

But Robert E. Lee did not like to think about this kind of thing. He was a soldier. And soon he would be a father. To him the important things were his duty to the Army and his duty to his family.

The Army sent Robert to work in Washington. Now the Lees could live at Arlington. Robert often had to be away. But he was always glad to come home to his growing family. In these years the Lees had seven children.

Robert E. Lee was a soldier, but he had never fought a battle. Then in 1846 war broke out between Mexico and the United States. Lee was sent to fight. He said good-by to Mary and the children. He was off to war.

5
The Mexican War

The big guns were ready. Captain Robert E. Lee had told the soldiers where to put them. He had made the men dig banks of dirt to hide behind.

Lee was helping General Winfield Scott plan a great battle. The Army was about to attack Vera Cruz, a large Mexican town on the sea.

The attack began. Soldiers fired the great guns at the walls of Vera Cruz. One of the men at the guns was Robert's brother, Smith Lee. When he could, Lee went to stand by his brother's gun. "I could see his white teeth through all the smoke of the fire," Lee said in a letter to Mary.

The Mexicans soon gave up Vera Cruz. General Scott thanked Lee for his work. Now the Army could move on to the Mexican capital.

The march to Mexico City would be hard. General Scott asked Lee to find the best way to go. And he asked him to see what Santa Anna, the Mexican general, was doing.

To get news for Scott, Lee went behind the lines of enemy soldiers. This was dangerous work.

Once when Lee was behind enemy lines he heard voices. Mexican soldiers were coming to drink at a spring! Lee jumped under a log. More Mexicans came. They sat on the log and talked. Lee had to hide there until dark.

Lee found out many things for Scott. Once he even found a secret road for the Army. And he was very brave. At Cerro Gordo he led the first line of men into battle. The Americans won. But Lee wrote to his son, Custis, "You have no idea what a horrible sight a field of battle is."

Then came the biggest battle of the war. The Americans attacked a fort outside Mexico City. Lee planned the attack. For days he worked without sleep. He found out where the Mexican soldiers were. He knew where to put the big guns. It was easy for the Army to take the fort. The American Army marched right into Mexico City. The war was over!

6
Back To West Point

Robert E. Lee came home. He had not seen Arlington or his family for two years. He hugged Mary and the children. But he could not find his youngest son Robert. "Where is my little boy?" he asked. A boy stood near by. Lee picked him up and kissed him. Everyone laughed. Lee had kissed his son's best friend.

The family was glad Lee was back. He high-jumped with the older boys. He had the littlest children tickle his feet while he told them stories. Sometimes the stories were so good the children forgot to tickle. "No tickling, no story," Lee would say.

The Army was pleased with Lee's work. They made him a colonel. They asked him to be head of West Point.

Colonel Lee liked running West Point. His oldest son Custis was a cadet now. Custis often visited him.

West Point was in New York, in the North. But the Lees felt at home there. Many of Colonel Lee's Army friends were from the North. Cadets from North and South were friends.

But there was bad feeling growing between North and South. The biggest reason for this was slavery.

Most people knew that slavery was wrong. In the North it was against the law. But in the South it was allowed. People with big farms said they needed slaves to do the work.

Lee knew that slavery was wrong. He said it was bad for the slave and worse for the man who owned him. He freed the few slaves his family had given him. When some said they wanted to go to Africa, he sent them.

Lee did not tell other people to free their slaves. And he thought the North had no right to tell the South what to do about slavery.

Lee did not like to argue about slavery. He thought it made the trouble worse. He did not see how deeply people felt.

In a few years Colonel Lee's job at West Point was over. The family was glad to get back to Virginia. But Lee had to leave often. He came home when he could. Old Mr. Custis had died. Now Lee had to run Arlington.

One fall day in 1859, a soldier came to Arlington. He carried a message for Colonel Lee.

Fighting had broken out in a town called Harpers Ferry in Virginia. Strangers with guns had come to free the slaves. Lee was told to bring Harpers Ferry to order.

Harpers Ferry: October, 1859

A great crowd had come to the firehouse. The men who had tried to free the slaves were hiding inside.

Colonel Lee sent a message in. He said soldiers were all around the building. He told the men to give up.

The men would not come out. They moved fire engines across the door.

The soldiers smashed in the door with a ladder. There were gunshots. A soldier fell. The rest ran in. Inside they found a band of men led by a strange, wild man.

This brave, angry man was John Brown. He hated slavery. Many in the North thought he was right in fighting to free the slaves. But in the South people hated him. Robert E. Lee believed he was a madman.

In December, 1859, John Brown was hanged. Robert E. Lee was there.

7 North Against South

On November 6, 1860, Americans elected a new President. He was a tall, thin man who had often spoken against slavery. His name was Abraham Lincoln.

People in the South were very unhappy. They did not want Lincoln for their President. Some Southern states said they did not want to be part of the United States any more. They voted to leave the Union. They joined to make a new country, the Confederate States of America. They chose their own president.

He was Jefferson Davis.

The Confederates knew Lincoln might fight to keep the country together. They asked Lee to be a general in their army. Lee said no. He thought states had no right to leave the Union. He hoped Virginia would not do it. "If Virginia stands by the Union, so will I," he said.

In the South, Confederates began taking over United States forts.

Lincoln said the South had to stay in the Union. He said the forts must be given back. But in April, 1861, Confederates fired on Fort Sumter in South Carolina. War had begun.

It was a hard time for Robert E. Lee. President Lincoln wanted him to lead the Union Army. Again, Lee said no. Virginia might join the Confederacy. Lee could never lead an army against his own state. He loved the United States. But he felt his first duty was to Virginia. He could not forget his father's words, "Virginia is my country."

Lee left the United States Army. He said he would not fight again unless Virginia needed him.

On April 17 Virginia joined the Confederacy. Lee was asked to lead Virginia's army. He could not say no.

He went to Richmond, the capital of Virginia. The city was crowded.

Men from all over the state had come to join the army. They were sure the South would win. They said the war would be short and glorious.

Lee did not think so. The North had more guns and men. Lincoln would fight hard to save the Union.

Lee had to get his men ready. He had to dig defenses. Digging was not glorious. People said he was afraid. They called him "Granny Lee."

Richmond became the Confederate capital. Jefferson Davis thought the Union Army might attack the city. He told Lee to protect Richmond.

Robert E. Lee was still there when the first battle of the American Civil War was fought.

Bull Run: July 21, 1861

Into Virginia marched 30,000 Union soldiers. They attacked an army of 20,000 Confederates. The two armies fought by a stream called Bull Run.

Fighting was fierce. But the Union army was winning. Then 9,000 more Confederates arrived. Most ran into battle. But General Thomas Jackson led his men to the top of a hill.

“Steady Men!” Jackson cried. “Hold your fire until they’re on you. And when you charge, yell like furies.” The Union soldiers attacked again. Confederate soldiers fell back. On came the Union men, their flags and guns shining in the sun.

Then down the hill came Jackson’s men, screaming the strange “Rebel yell.” Union soldiers were terrified. They threw down their guns and ran.

The Confederacy had won the first battle! Jackson was a hero! Soldiers said he had stood “like a stone wall.” They called him Stonewall Jackson. For now, General Lee was forgotten.

8 The Army of Northern Virginia

Robert E. Lee and Jefferson Davis rode toward the sound of the battle. Bull Run had been a great victory for the South. But since then things had gone badly. Confederate armies had lost many battles in the West. And now a Union army was just a few miles from Richmond.

For a year Lee had been helping Davis plan the war. This was the first battle he had seen.

The road was filled with wounded soldiers leaving the battle. Just then a wounded man was carried by. It was the Confederate general.

Now the army needed a new leader.

On the way back to Richmond, Jefferson Davis turned to Robert E. Lee. He asked him to lead the army.

In June, 1862, General Lee became the leader of the Confederate Army of Northern Virginia.

The men in Lee's army were from all over the South. Some were rich men who brought their own guns and horses. Most were poor farm boys.

Lee tried to get to know his men.

He often went among them. The men looked forward to seeing their tall, handsome leader ride by on his great gray horse, Traveler. Lee made his men work hard. But he was always fair with them. And the men came to love him.

Lee's army was much smaller than the Union army. He knew it would be hard to push the Union army away from Richmond. But he had a plan.

Most of the time Confederate armies had waited for Union armies to attack. This time Lee was going to attack first.

The attack began. Again and again the Confederates charged. Again and again they were beaten back.

Stonewall Jackson and his men arrived. "That fire is very heavy," said Lee. "Do you think your men can stand it?"

"They can stand almost anything," said Jackson. Into battle they went.

Still the Confederates could not push the Union men back. Lee turned to General John B. Hood. He asked him to lead a charge.

Ahead of Hood's men was a hill. There, three lines of Union riflemen waited. On top of the hill were Union cannons. Hood charged. The rifles cracked. The cannons roared. Many of Hood's men fell. But the rest kept coming. They did not yell. They did not fire. They just ran.

Up the hill they came. The Union soldiers dropped their guns and ran. Then Hood's men fired. Union soldiers fell everywhere.

The Union army had been pushed back. Lee had won his first battle.

Lee drove the Union army away from Richmond. Now he had to push it out of Virginia.

Lee's soldiers wore rags. Some had no guns or shoes. They needed food. Union armies had guns and food. But still Lee won battle after battle.

Lee's "scarecrow army" fought bravely. And their general planned battles well. In the South he was a hero. Even in the North people said he was the best general in the war.

9
Chancellorsville

Union soldiers were talking and playing cards. The sun was going down. The soldiers were sure Lee and Jackson would not attack today.

The dinner call came. Soldiers put away their guns and went to eat.

Just then deer jumped out of the woods and ran by. Rabbits hopped out after them. The men laughed and cheered.

Suddenly rifle shots came from the woods. The cheering stopped.

Out of the forest rushed Stonewall Jackson's men, yelling as they came.

The Union soldiers ran in terror.

To the east, Stonewall heard the sound of firing. Lee was attacking the other side of the Union army. Lee's battle plan was working well.

The moon rose. Jackson wanted to see if the time was right for another attack. He and a few men rode ahead. They saw that the Union men were still running. They turned back toward the Confederate army.

Suddenly there were shots. The Confederates were firing at them! They thought Jackson's men were Union soldiers. Jackson was hit!

The next day General Lee rode through the battlefield. When his soldiers saw him, they began to cheer. The cheering grew and grew.

It had been General Lee's greatest battle. The Union army was twice as big as his. But he and Stonewall had beaten it. It should have been a great day for Lee. But he was very sad. Many brave men had died. And in a little house a few miles away, his best general lay badly wounded.

At first Jackson seemed to get better. But this did not last. One afternoon, in a fever, he began to call out orders to his men. Then he stopped and smiled. "Let us cross over the river," he said, "and rest under the shade of the trees." And then he died.

The death of Stonewall Jackson was a terrible loss to General Lee.

10
Gettysburg

General Lee decided to fight in the North. He led his men into Pennsylvania. They met a Union army near the town of Gettysburg.

This was not where Lee wanted to fight. It was not a battle he had planned. But he knew that if he won here, he might win the war.

After two days of fighting, Lee decided it was time for a great attack. He rode out to see his men. This time they could not cheer him. That would show the Union army where they were. But as he passed, they quietly took off their hats.

The Confederates were hidden behind some trees. In front of them were open fields. Across the fields was a line of hills. There the Union army waited.

Out of the woods the Confederates charged. But this time the Union men did not run. They fired and kept on firing. Thousands of brave Confederates died in that terrible charge. The rest were driven back.

A great cheer went up from the Union lines. They had beaten Lee!

The next day a heavy rain began to fall. Sad and tired, Lee took his army back to Virginia.

Now the North was sure it could win the war. And Lincoln thought he had found the man to do it. This general had beaten the Confederate armies in the West. His name was Ulysses S. Grant.

In May, 1864 Grant was ready.

A huge Union army moved toward Richmond. Lee was waiting. Grant lost 60,000 men in three terrible battles. Lee lost half that many. But Grant did not give up.

Grant marched south. He planned to attack Richmond from the other side. But Lee hurried to stop him.

To reach Richmond, Grant had to get by the town of Petersburg. There Lee met him. Line after line of Union soldiers charged Lee's army. But Lee held them off. Still Grant did not give up. Lee's army was in Petersburg, and Grant was not going to let it get away. He was going to keep on attacking until General Lee was beaten for good.

11
The Fall of the Army of Northern Virginia

"General, I have no shoes," said a soldier. "I haven't enough to eat," said another. Lee rode sadly among his men. His brave army had just pushed Grant back again. But the men could not last much longer.

It was the winter of 1865. For months Lee's army had been under attack in Petersburg. Union cannons had fired without stop. Union men had even dug a tunnel under Lee's lines and exploded a huge bomb. Still Lee's men held Grant off.

Grant lost thousands of men. But he could get more. Lee could not.

By now Lee's army was half as big as Grant's. And many of his best generals had been killed.

Lee's men were weak from hunger. Many were barefoot in the snow. Many were sick. Some soldiers could stand no more and ran away. But most of the ragged little army kept on fighting.

The men loved Lee. They would fight as long as he asked them to.

Grant attacked again and again. Lee saw that he could not save Richmond. He had to escape.

General Lee led his men out of Petersburg. He marched them toward a small town by a railroad. From there they could move by train out of Virginia. They would join a Confederate army in North Carolina. Then they could attack Grant again.

But Grant and his men followed Lee out of Petersburg.

Lee had ordered food for the army. But when the soldiers arrived in the town, no food was there.

Lee led his starving army south.

Grant's army followed close behind.

On April 6 Union soldiers caught up. They attacked. That night only 15,000 men were left in Lee's army. But still they tramped on. Grant and 80,000 men came after them.

Lee wanted to reach Appomattox Station. Food trains were waiting there. He could feed his army and escape. But by the time the army arrived, Union armies were all around the town. Lee was trapped.

When Virginia had gone to war Lee had agreed to fight. But now he saw that his state would be ruined if the fighting went on. Most of his men would be killed. It was time to give up the fight. He would surrender.

Appomattox: April 9, 1865

Ulysses S. Grant never looked like a great general. Today his beard was wild. His clothes were muddy from a long ride. He entered the farmhouse.

Inside was a man in a fine uniform. A beautiful sword hung by his side. It was General Robert E. Lee.

The two men shook hands. They sat down and General Grant wrote out the surrender. It was very fair. General Lee signed it.

As General Lee left, Grant and his men raised their hats in salute.

Lee rode back to his army. Sadly he told his men he had given up. The men crowded around Traveler to give their general a last cheer. They reached out to touch his hand. One soldier cried, "I love you just as well as ever, General Lee." Tears were in Lee's eyes as he rode away.

12
The Last Years

Robert E. Lee had led the people of the South through the war. They would still turn to him for help in the hard years that followed. He told them to forget the war. He said they should work to build up their country again.

A Confederate soldier told Lee he wanted to leave America. "Do not leave Virginia," Lee begged. "Our country needs her young men now."

Everyone wanted to see what Lee would do. He was offered many jobs. But he turned them all down. Then he was asked to be the president of a small college in Lexington, Virginia. He said yes. He wanted to lead young men of the South in peace as he had led them in war.

Lee loved his work at Washington College. He knew all the students.

He was kind and fair with them, as he had been with his soldiers. And like his soldiers, they loved him.

The college had been badly hurt by the war. Many buildings were ruined. When Lee came, there were only four teachers and 45 students.

Lee worked hard. He got people to give money. And the college grew.

The Lees had their own house near the college. And General Lee could ride Traveler in the hills around Lexington. Life was happy for the first time in many years.

By 1866 there was a new law in the United States. No state could allow slavery. Lee was very glad. He said he "rejoiced" when the law passed.

In 1870 Lee was 63. But he looked much older. Long years of war and hard work at the college had tired him. He was not well. Friends said he should go away to a warm place. In March he set off on a long trip through the South.

People from all over the South came to see their great hero. They crowded at train stations when he came through. Old friends and soldiers from his army came. People brought babies named after him.

Lee visited his father's grave on an island off Georgia. He stayed with cousins and friends. Then he moved slowly back through Virginia. He came home in May, very tired.

Lee was not well that fall. One wet afternoon he went to a church meeting. It was cold and damp. He sat wrapped in an old army coat.

When Lee came home, he was very weak and had to be put to bed. His doctor came. He told Lee to hurry and get well. He said Traveler would get fat with no one to ride him.

But General Lee would never ride Traveler again. For a week the old soldier lay in bed. Mrs. Lee stayed near him. One day he began to call out to his soldiers. Then on October 12, 1870, he said softly, "Strike the tent." He was telling his men to take down his tent. Those were his last words. General Lee was dead.

The Funeral of General Lee

The band played a slow, sad march. Once every minute a cannon boomed.

Through Lexington marched soldiers and students, the men Robert E. Lee had led in war and in peace.

Two soldiers led Traveler. The tall, gray horse had carried General Lee over battlefields and quiet hills. His saddle was on his back. But today he had no rider.

13
After Robert E. Lee

He was a simple man. He loved his family and Virginia. He had a simple faith in God. And he always did what he thought was his duty.

Robert E. Lee was the last great man of old Virginia. In many ways he was closer to his hero, George Washington, than he was to men of his own time.

Washington College was named after George Washington. After Lee died, the college was given a new name. It was called Washington and Lee.

The STEP-UP Books

NATURE LIBRARY

ANIMALS DO THE STRANGEST THINGS

BIRDS DO THE STRANGEST THINGS

FISH DO THE STRANGEST THINGS

INSECTS DO THE STRANGEST THINGS

Story of AMERICA

Meet THE NORTH AMERICAN INDIANS

Meet THE MEN WHO SAILED THE SEAS

Meet CHRISTOPHER COLUMBUS

Meet THE PILGRIM FATHERS

Meet BENJAMIN FRANKLIN

Meet GEORGE WASHINGTON

Meet THOMAS JEFFERSON

THE ADVENTURES OF LEWIS AND CLARK

Meet ANDREW JACKSON

Meet ABRAHAM LINCOLN

Meet ROBERT E. LEE

Meet THEODORE ROOSEVELT

Meet JOHN F. KENNEDY

THE STORY OF FLIGHT

THE WAY THE COUNTRY

FROM 1861

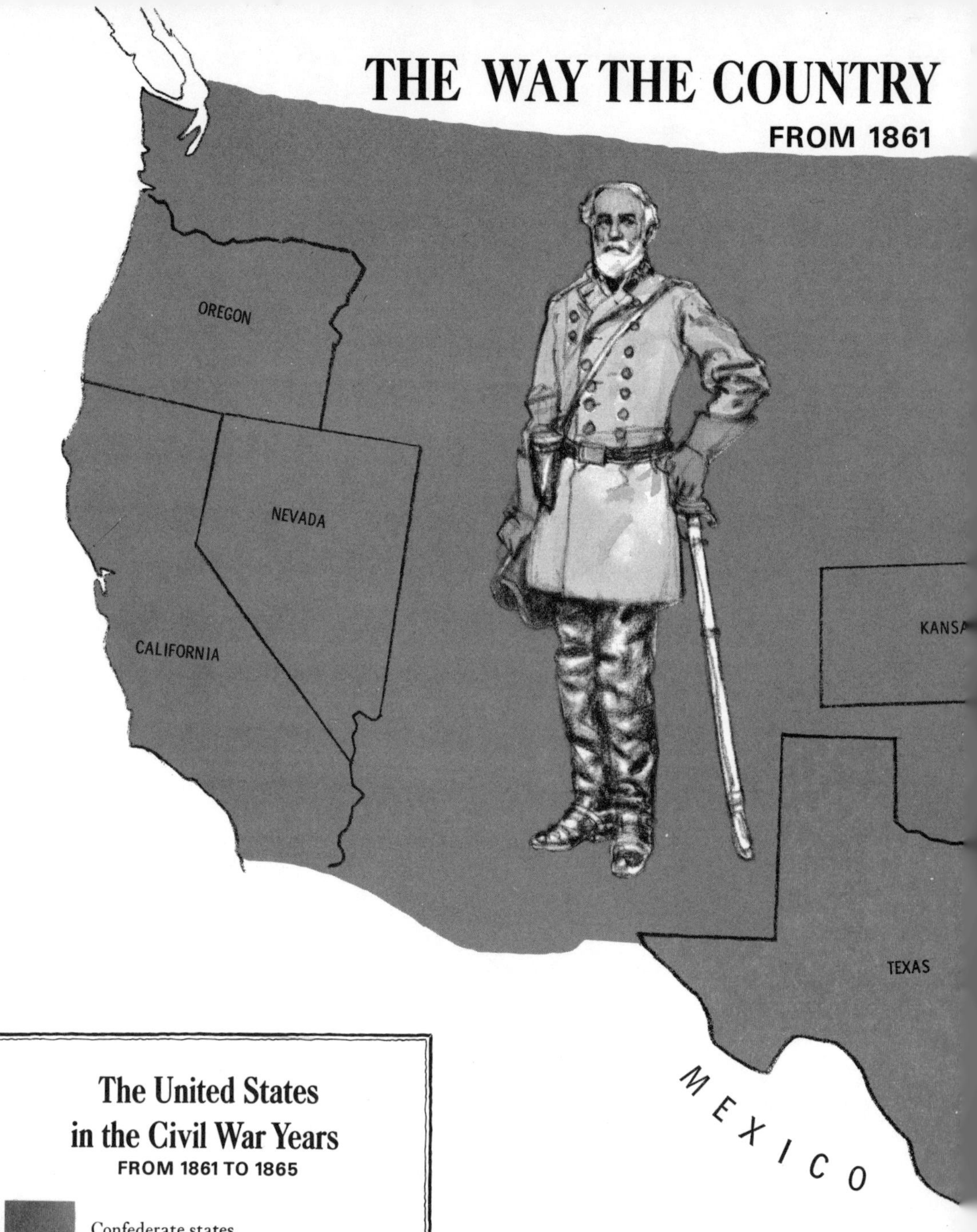

The United States in the Civil War Years

FROM 1861 TO 1865

Confederate states.

★ Important places in the life of Robert E. Lee